CHRISTIAN ROSENKREUTZ

POCKET LIBRARY OF SPIRITUAL WISDOM

Also available
ALCHEMY
ATLANTIS
THE DRUIDS
THE GODDESS
THE HOLY GRAIL

The mystic seven-petalled rose as a symbol of the seven planets, the cosmic transmutation-process, etc. The cross-structure of the stem alludes to the Christian meaning of that process for the self in the modern age. Rudolf Steiner based many meditations around this fundamental symbol of the cosmic meaning of Christianity, the rediscovery of which is one central thread of his anthroposophy ('human wisdom'). Rosicrucian symbol from Joachim Frizius, Summum Bonum.

CHRISTIAN ROSENKREUTZ

The Mystery, Teaching and Mission of a Master

selections from the work of

RUDOLF STEINER

Sophia Books

All translations revised by Christian von Arnim

Sophia Books
An imprint of Rudolf Steiner Press
Hillside House, The Square
Forest Row, East Sussex
RH18 5ES

www.rudolfsteinerpress.com

Published by Rudolf Steiner Press 2001

Series editor: Andrew Welburn
For earlier English publications of extracted material see p. 79

The material by Rudolf Steiner was originally published in German
in various volumes of the 'GA' (*Rudolf Steiner Gesamtausgabe* or
Collected Works) by Rudolf Steiner Verlag, Dornach. This
authorized edition is published by permission of the Rudolf Steiner
Nachlassverwaltung, Dornach (for further information see p. 84)

A catalogue record for this book is available from the British Library

ISBN 1 85584 084 7

Cover illustration by Anne Stockton. Cover design by
Andrew Morgan
Typeset by DP Photosetting, Aylesbury, Bucks.
Printed and bound in Great Britain by Cromwell Press Limited,
Trowbridge, Wilts.

Contents

Introduction: The Rosicrucian Dimension in the Work of Rudolf Steiner

by Andrew J. Welburn

Early in the seventeenth century, a number of strange, not to say startling booklets were printed in Germany concerning a mysterious Brotherhood 'of the Rosy Cross', causing what is still often termed the Rosicrucian furore. The first was the *Fama Fraternitatis* (sometimes translated 'Fame', but used in the old Latin sense of a report, a making something known); this was followed by the *Confessio*, or 'admission', so to speak, by the Brotherhood of their existence and their role. And there was a long, beautifully told alchemical fable, *The Chymical Wedding*. Addressed by way of a challenge to the 'learned of Europe', they intimated that the Brotherhood was in possession of both religious and 'philosophical' (i.e. scientific, notably alchemical) secrets, and that it could solve many of the problems which faced that turbulent time. All three of the 'manifestos' referred furthermore to a great adept-founder of the Brotherhood, who himself bore the name of Rosy-Cross, or Christian Rosenkreutz.

It was the first occasion on which either the existence of the mysterious Rosicrucian Brotherhood or of its founder Christian Rosenkreutz were mentioned to the world at large. For the most part, the world at large has ever since regarded both of them as a fiction; and many organizations which have claimed to be the one and know something of the other have come and gone over the centuries since, often casting little further light.[1]

Yet the Rosicrucians have a way of turning up in connection with many great thinkers and spiritual teachers, or creative writers and dramatists, or issues such as the relationship between science and spirituality, which still have the power to change our modern world. Behind the riddle of this 'Invisible College' in fact stands a figure who must be regarded as a guiding spirit of the modern age. But we are likely to misunderstand his guiding role and the nature of his mission unless we are aware of the direction in which his teaching leads, turning him into just another spiritual 'authority', or purveyor of a secret doctrine to a closed circle of his disciples. Christian Rosenkreutz is much more than any of these things, and it is Rudolf Steiner who can tell us of the larger dimension behind his appearance and place in spiritual evolution—not least because Steiner himself played a part in the furtherance of the Rosicrucian mission to bring spiritual knowledge to people in today's world, in a manner compatible with modern thinking and inner freedom.

Christian Rosenkreutz, according to the traditional sources such as the Rosicrucian *Confessio*, lived from 1378 to 1504. But the real effect of his teaching, represented symbolically as the 'opening of his tomb', is felt only a century later, from 1604. This already indicates that what is important about him is not just his teaching, but rather a special relationship to the needs of different times, so that he is among those who prepare the future—not one who works directly in the present. The sources indicate this further by associating him with the prophetic teachings of the Book of Revelation and its author John, and also with the Gospel of John; it is said of him that he beholds heaven opening, with the angels descending (John 1:51 cf. Rev. 19:11), and the names written in the book of life (Rev. 3:5). The description of his tomb meanwhile is filled with further secret symbolism, his miraculous preservation when the tomb is opened above all suggestive of Egyptian and Hermetic Mysteries, such as were undoubtedly important among the Rosicrucian brothers.

> The everlasting taper lights the gloom;
> All wisdom shut into his onyx eyes
> Our Father Rosicross sleeps in his tomb

as the poet W.B. Yeats was later beautifully to imagine the mystic scene.[2]

But it would be wrong therefore simply to equate the Rosicrucians with the widespread 'Hermetic revival' of the seventeenth century, or to deny them any real earlier roots as does, for instance, the influential historian Frances Yates.[3] Though the account is certainly meant to indicate Hermetic-Egyptian Mysteries, we should recall that once again it is John who, according to Christian legend, 'sleeps in his tomb' until Christ comes again—in Ephesus, which was another centre of spiritual Mysteries in the ancient world.[4] The message is not just that Christian Rosenkreutz is in possession of Mystery-secrets, but even more that he is a key to the Christian understanding of them, in an apocalyptic context that points to a renewal of Christian teaching—the new 'Reformation of the whole wide world' to which the Rosicrucian literature refers.

As ancient Hermetic knowledge was turning into modern science, then, in the early seventeenth century, what the Rosicrucian *fratres* revealed to the world from the teachings of the Founder was an ideal of 'pansophia', or universal wisdom that was Christian and spiritual yet drawn from the same Mystery-sources as Hermeticism itself. It was the step forward in the deepening of Christian understanding which might have still prevented the divorce between science and spirituality, and indeed did prevent it to a considerable extent until Darwin, through the profound influence which these ideas are now known to have had on Isaac Newton. The spiritual-magical dimension of knowledge was still grasped by the early Newtonians, and the esoteric aspects of it were propagated in the secret societies and Freemasonry of the eighteenth century.[5] And once again Rudolf Steiner's work needs to be seen in this Rosicrucian context; for in the evolutionary, post-Darwinian context he saw the way to develop also a new form of spiritual science. As Darwinism threatened to reduce humanity to mere animals, it was Steiner who showed that it was possible not to reject science, but to evolve along with it, as its counterpart and spiritual dimension, an 'anthroposophia'—anthroposophy, as it is usually rendered in English—or 'wisdom of humanity'. This was in a profound way, as Rudolf Steiner himself showed in many of his books and cycles of lectures, a fulfilment that was required at our later stage of those same Rosicrucian ideals.[6]

Those ideals extend, however, far beyond a concern with science and scientific special ideas. For the rise of science is no more than a symptom of a larger change in consciousness, which has been coming about over longer epochs of cultural and spiritual evolution. It is part of the impulse of ego-consciousness, leading humanity to experience the freedom to think for itself, to question and find answers for itself, which affects all spheres of life—the social and the spiritual as well as the intellectual. 'For in working actively upon nature,' Rudolf Steiner pointed out,

> the soul is consciously experiencing its own essential life. As a living experience, this activity is very much more than merely gathering so much information about nature. It is an evolution of the self that is experienced in building up the scientific picture of nature...
>
> One often hears it said that works on occult science contain no proofs of what they bring forward, merely making statements that are said to be the teaching of occult science. It would be a mistake to think that what is said here has been advanced in this spirit. Our purpose at any rate is different. It is to encourage what is developed in the human soul through the knowledge of nature to go on evolving, as it can do, through its own inherent power. We may then point to the fact that on its path of further evolution the soul will encounter realities beyond those of the

senses. Our premise is that everyone who reads this, and is able to follow such a course, is bound to meet with these realities.[7]

It is because the underlying attitude to modern knowledge has changed, and needs to be recognized also in its spiritual dimension, that the form in which the wisdom of Christian Rosenkreutz was communicated could not simply be a continuation of the older Mystery-forms. It is because he could foresee this and prepare the way for new forms of Mystery-wisdom, indeed, that Christian Rosenkreutz must be acknowledged as one of the greatest spiritual leaders. He is represented in the Rosicrucian tradition as actually the 'guardian' of modern spiritual truth in the form it can be communicated, in freedom, to those who are ready to receive it.

Along the path to knowledge of higher realities as it evolves in the soul, one might therefore say, one will also inevitably meet with Christian Rosenkreutz, though it need not be in any obvious way or in any formal relation of discipleship. In this book we will find Rudolf Steiner describing how the modern path is one where we may learn to look for the help and guidance of Christian Rosenkreutz — if we also learn how to recognize it. The early Rosicrucians did not work in the old manner of the Mysteries, when pupils had to withdraw from the world to special sites where such matters could be communicated. They formed an 'Invisible College', not set apart but moving among the people and bringing their insight to bear where it was needed. (There is a certain irony in the fact that among those who later developed a paranoia about 'secret societies' the Rosicrucians, with their more outward-looking attitude, came to represent that threat in its direst form.) The poet Goethe, who knew much about genuine Rosicrucianism, Freemasonry and alchemy, hinted symbolically at the change in his poetic fragment *The Mysteries* and in his fascinating 'fairy-tale' of *The Green Snake and Beautiful Lily*. In the first he tells how Christian Rosenkreutz had once learned the universal wisdom of the old Mystery-centres; in the second he described how the Rosicrucian secret temple of the 'metallic kings' (i.e., containing the forces of spiritual-alchemical transmutation), which had formerly been concealed in the depths of the earth, would one day rise up into the light of day. This theme too can be traced in Rudolf Steiner's work, for example in his conception of the Goetheanum building which houses the Anthroposophical Society and is its spiritual centre; this can be understood as in form a 'subterranean' Rosicrucian temple such as the one Rudolf Steiner designed in Malsch, but now bringing its Mystery-teaching into the open, into the world of conscious striving and knowing.[8] In its dominating position, yet intimate relationship to the shaping forces of the surrounding landscape, to the earthly and the heavenly worlds, it embodies a typically 'Rosicrucian' gesture.

The Rosicrucian focus in Steiner's work also helps explain his involvement with certain esoteric groups who were also, from various directions, working to fulfil the Rosicrucian ideal. It was an essential part of his work to bring esoteric knowledge into modern life. It is well known that he

acquired a charter to perform certain 'Memphis and Mis-
raim', i.e., Egyptian-inspired, ceremonies which were used
in circles of high-grade Masonry — although he did not in
reality employ it to perform any traditional Masonic rites.[9]
We may see here rather something in the spirit of the Rosicrucian 'Egyptian' or Hermetic symbolism from the *Confessio*. Steiner was also involved with the Rosicrucian Order
which had inspired Yeats's poem which we quoted earlier,
and tried especially with the collaboration of H. Collison to
help them in the direction of his own Rosicrucian knowledge.[10] The proper relationship to the 'Masters', as the
Theosophists had come to call them, was frequently a central
issue. The search for the Masters had assumed many forms
already in the spiritual movements of the time — and it may
be said that it could be both a help and a hindrance. In its
highest form, it might be the search for the true sources of
knowledge and insight. At its worst, it could become a
destructive quest for outside 'authorities' that actually got in
the way of any serious efforts in spiritual development, or
turn into the pseudo-Messianism and ultimate fiasco of the
Order of the Star of the East. Rudolf Steiner too had taught,
during the earlier phases of his work, in the name of the
traditional Masters of Wisdom.[11] But in accordance with the
Rosicrucian principle, as he developed his 'anthroposophical' approach, he had sought to enable his pupils to
find a firm foundation in the nature of spiritual knowledge
itself, not in the authority of hidden Masters.

The immediate benefit of such an approach in the modern
world, Steiner argued, was that it

can be achieved by individuals themselves, where the initiator merely gives indications about what ought to be done, and one then gradually learns to find one's own way forward. No considerable progress has yet been made along this path; but little by little there will unfold in humanity a faculty making it possible for a person both to ascend into the macrocosm and descend into the micro-cosm without assistance and to pass through these forms of initiation as a free being.[12]

But there were also deeper reasons—connected with the whole mission of Christian Rosenkreutz and esoteric Chris-tianity. For this tentative new form of spiritual awareness will bring a renewal of mankind's relationship to Christ, which Rudolf Steiner describes as an awareness of his pre-sence—the *parousia*—not physically now, but in the 'etheric' or life-sphere of the earth. That revelation, however, will come in many separate facets, through personal and indivi-dual insights into the working of the living Christ—and it is ultimately for that reason that esoteric development must now take a free and individual form. To put together our different esoteric insights, building up the mystical body of Christ and preparing the spiritual consciousness we need to heal the living earth, is the task of the future.[13] This little book brings together some of Rudolf Steiner's most sig-nificant statements about this process, and how we can find its connection with the mission of Christian Rosenkreutz.

1. The Mystery of Christian Rosenkreutz

The identity of Christian Rosenkreutz has always been shrouded in mystery, and in this first lecture-presentation Rudolf Steiner reveals why. The nature and work of Christian Rosenkreutz cannot be understood in terms of one incarnation alone. Hitherto the sources of Rosicrucian knowledge have therefore been made known only to the initiated, or in veiled imaginative form as in Goethe's poem The Mysteries. *But knowledge of the hidden side of human life is needed nowadays for humanity's evolution; Christian Rosenkreutz is the guide to its significance and to the 'Christ Event starting in the twentieth century' in which it will enable us to share.*

Christian Rosenkreutz is an individual who is active both when he is in incarnation and when he is not incarnated in a physical body; he works not only as a physical being and through physical forces, but above all spiritually, through higher forces.

As we know, man lives not only for himself but also in connection with human evolution as a whole. Usually when someone passes through death his etheric body dissolves into the cosmos.[14] A part of this dissolving etheric body always stays intact, however, and so we are always surrounded by these remaining parts of the etheric bodies of the dead, for our good or also to our detriment. They affect us for good or ill according to whether we ourselves are good or bad. Far-reaching effects emanate also from the etheric bodies of great individualities. Great forces emanating from the etheric body of Christian Rosenkreutz can work into our soul and also into our spirit. It is our duty to get to know these forces, for we work with them as Rosicrucians. Strictly speaking, the Rosicrucian movement began in the thirteenth century. At that time these forces worked extraordinarily strongly, and a Christian Rosenkreutz stream has been active in spiritual life ever since. There is a law that this spiritual stream of force has to become especially powerful every hundred years or so. This can be seen now in the theosophical movement. Christian Rosenkreutz himself gave an indication of this in his last exoteric statements.[15]

In 1785, the collected esoteric revelations of the Rosicrucians appeared in the work *The Secret Symbols of the Rosicrucians* by Hinricus Madathanus Theosophus.[16] In a certain limited sense this publication contains references to the Rosicrucian stream active in the previous century, which was revealed for the first time in the works collected and put together by Hinricus Madathanus Theosophus. Another hundred years later we see the influence of the Rosicrucian stream coming to expression again in the work of H.P. Blavatsky, especially in the book *Isis Unveiled*. A considerable amount of Western occult wisdom is contained in this book that is still a long way from being improved upon, even though the composition is sometimes very confused. It is interesting to compare *The Secret Symbols of the Rosicrucians* by Hinricus Madathanus Theosophus with the works of H.P. Blavatsky. We must think especially of the first part of the publication, which is written in 'symbolic' form. In the second part Blavatsky deviates a little from the Rosicrucian stream. In her later works she departs entirely from it, and we must be able to distinguish between her early and her later publications, even though something of her uncritical spirit already appears in the early ones. That this is said is no more than the wish of H.P. Blavatsky herself, who is not in incarnation now.

When we look at the characteristic quality of human consciousness in the thirteenth century, we see that primitive clairvoyance had gradually disappeared. We know that in earlier times everybody had an elementary clairvoyance. In the middle of the thirteenth century this reached its lowest point, and there was suddenly no more clairvoyance. Everyone experienced a spiritual eclipse. Even the most enlightened spirits and the most highly developed individuals, including initiates, had no further access to the spiritual worlds, and when they spoke about the spiritual worlds they had to confine themselves to what remained in their memories. People only knew about the spiritual world from tradition or from those initiates who awakened their memories of what they had previously experienced. For a short time, though, even these minds could not see directly into the spiritual world.

This short period of darkness had to take place at that time to prepare for what is characteristic of our present age — today's intellectual, rational development. That is what is important today in the fifth post-Atlantean cultural epoch.[17] In the Graeco-Roman cultural epoch, the development of the intellect was not as it is today. Direct perception was the vital factor, not intellectual thinking. Human beings identified with what they saw and heard, in fact even with what they thought. They did not produce thoughts from out of themselves then as we do today, and as we ought to do, for this is the task of the fifth post-Atlantean cultural epoch. People's clairvoyance gradually begins again after this time, and the clairvoyance of the future can now develop.

The Rosicrucian stream began in the thirteenth century. During that century, individuals particularly suitable for initiation had to be specially chosen. Initiation could take place only after the short period of darkness had run its course.

In a place in Europe that cannot be named[18] — though this will be possible in the not very distant future — a lodge of a very spiritual nature was formed comprising a council of twelve men who had received into themselves the sum of the spiritual wisdom of olden times and of their own time. Thus we are concerned with twelve men who lived in that dark era, twelve outstanding individualities, who united to help the progress of humanity. None of them could see directly into the spiritual world, but they could awaken to life in themselves memories of what they had experienced through earlier initiations. And the karma of humankind brought it about that everything that still remained to humankind of the ancient Atlantean epoch was incarnated in seven of these twelve. In my *An Outline of Esoteric Science* it has already been

stated that in the seven holy rishis of old, the teachers of the
ancient Indian cultural epoch, all that was left of the Atlantean epoch was preserved.[19] These seven men who were
incarnated again in the thirteenth century, and who were
part of the council of twelve, were those who could look back
into the seven streams of the ancient Atlantean cultural
epoch of mankind and the further course of these streams.

Each of these seven individualities could bring one stream
to life for their time and our present time. In addition to these
seven there were another four who could not look back into
times long past but could look back to the occult wisdom
mankind had acquired in the four post-Atlantean epochs.
The first could look back to the ancient Indian period, the
second to the ancient Iranian cultural period, the third to the
Egyptian-Mesopotamian-Assyrian-Babylonian cultural period and the fourth to Graeco-Roman culture. These four
joined the seven to form a council of wise men in the thirteenth century. A twelfth had the fewest memories as it were;
however, he was the most intellectual among them, and it
was his task to foster external science in particular. These
twelve individualities not only lived in the experiences of
Western esoteric knowledge, but these twelve different
streams of wisdom worked together to make a whole. A
remarkable reference to this can be found in Goethe's poem
The Mysteries.[20]

We shall be speaking, then, of twelve outstanding individualities. The middle of the thirteenth century is the time
when a new culture began. At this time a certain low point of
spiritual life had been reached. Even the most highly

developed could not approach the spiritual worlds. Then it was that the council of these most spiritually advanced people assembled. These twelve men, who represented the sum of all the spiritual knowledge of their age and the twelve schools of thought, came together in a place in Europe that cannot as yet be named.

This council of the twelve only possessed clairvoyant memory and intellectual wisdom. The seven successors of the seven rishis remembered their ancient wisdom, and the other five represented the wisdom of the five post-Atlantean cultures. Thus the twelve represented the whole of Atlantean and post-Atlantean wisdom. The twelfth was a man who attained the intellectual wisdom of his time in the highest degree. He possessed intellectually all the knowledge of his time, whilst the others, to whom direct spiritual wisdom was also then denied, acquired their knowledge by returning in memory to their earlier incarnations.

The beginning of a new culture was only possible, however, because a thirteenth came to join the twelve. The thirteenth did not become a scholar in the accepted sense of that time. He was an individuality who had been incarnated at the time of the Mystery of Golgotha. In the incarnations that followed, he prepared himself for his mission through humility of soul and through a fervent life devoted to God. He was a great soul, a pious, deeply mystical human being, who had not just acquired these qualities but was born with them. If you imagine a young man who is very pious and who devotes all his time to devout prayer to God, then you can have a picture of this thirteenth individuality.

He grew up entirely under the care and instruction of the twelve, and he received as much wisdom as each one could give him. He was educated with the greatest care, and every precaution was taken to see that no one other than the twelve exercised an influence on him. He was kept apart from the rest of the world. He was a very delicate child in that incarnation of the thirteenth century, and therefore the education that the twelve bestowed upon him worked right into his physical body. Now the twelve, being deeply devoted to their spiritual tasks and inwardly permeated with Christianity, were conscious that the external Christianity of the Church was only a caricature of real Christianity. They were permeated with the greatness of Christianity, although in the outside world they were regarded as its enemies. Each individuality worked his way into just one aspect of Christianity. Their endeavour was to unite the various religions into one great whole. They were convinced that the whole of spiritual life was contained in their twelve streams, and each one influenced the pupil to the best of his ability. Their aim was to achieve a synthesis of all the religions, but they knew that this was not to be achieved by means of any theory but only through active spiritual life. And for this a suitable education of the thirteenth was essential.

Whilst the spiritual forces of the thirteenth increased beyond measure, his physical forces drained away. It came to the point when he almost ceased to have any further connection with external life, and all interest in the physical world disappeared. He lived entirely for the sake of the spiritual development which the twelve were bringing about in him. The wisdom of the twelve was reflected in him. It reached the point where the thirteenth refused to eat and wasted away. Then an event occurred that could only happen once in history. It was the kind of event that can take place when the forces of the macrocosm co-operate for the sake of what they can bring to fruition. After a few days the body of the thirteenth became quite transparent, and for days he lay as though dead. The twelve now gathered round him at certain intervals. At these moments all knowledge and wisdom flowed from their lips. Whilst the thirteenth lay as though dead, they let their wisdom flow towards him in short prayer-like formulae. The best way to imagine them is to picture the twelve in a circle round the thirteenth.

This situation ended when the soul of the thirteenth awakened like a new soul. He had experienced a great transformation of soul. Within him there now existed something that was like a completely new birth of the twelve streams of wisdom, so that the twelve wise men could also learn something entirely new from the youth. His body, too, came to life in such a way that this revival of his absolutely transparent body was beyond compare. The youth could now speak of quite new experiences. The twelve recognized that he had experienced a repetition of the vision of Paul on the road to Damascus. In the course of a few weeks the thirteenth reproduced all the wisdom he had received from the twelve, but in a new form. This new form was as though given by Christ himself. What he now revealed to them, the twelve called true Christianity, the synthesis of all the religions, and they distinguished between this true Christianity and the Christianity of the period in which they lived. The thirteenth died relatively young, and the twelve then devoted themselves to the task of recording what the thirteenth had revealed to them, in imaginations — for it could only be done in that way. Thus the symbolic figures and images contained in the collection of Hinricus Madathanus Theosophus, and the communications of H.P. Blavatsky in the work *Isis Unveiled* arose. We have to see the occult process in such a way that the fruits of the initiation of the thirteenth remained within the spiritual atmosphere of the earth as the residue of his etheric body. This residue inspired the twelve as well as their pupils who succeeded them, so that they could form the occult Rosicrucian stream. Yet it continued to work as an etheric body, and it then became part of the new etheric body of the thirteenth when he incarnated again.

The individuality of the thirteenth reincarnated as early as half-way through the fourteenth century. In this incarnation he lived for over a hundred years. He was brought up in a similar way, in the circle of the pupils and successors of the twelve, but not so secluded as in his previous incarnation. When he was 28 years old he conceived a remarkable ideal. He had to leave Europe and travel. First he went to Damascus, and what Paul had experienced there happened again to him. This event can be described as the fruits of what took place in the previous incarnation. All the forces of the wonderful etheric body of the individuality of the thirteenth century had remained intact; none of them dispersed after death into the general world ether. This was a permanent etheric body, remaining intact in the ether spheres thereafter. This same highly spiritual etheric body again radiated from the spiritual world into the new incarnation of the individuality in the fourteenth century. That is why he was led to experience the event of Damascus again.

It is the individuality of Christian Rosenkreutz. He was the thirteenth in the circle of the twelve. He was named thus from this incarnation onwards. Esoterically, in the occult sense, he was already Christian Rosenkreutz in the thirteenth century, but exoterically he was named thus only from the fourteenth century. And the pupils of this thirteenth are the successors of the other twelve in the thirteenth century. These are the Rosicrucians.

At that time Christian Rosenkreutz travelled through the whole of the known world. After he had received all the wisdom of the twelve, fructified by the mighty Being of the Christ, it was easy for him to receive all the wisdom of that time in the course of seven years. When, after seven years, he returned to Europe, he took the most highly developed pupils and successors of the twelve as his pupils, and then began the actual work of the Rosicrucians.

By the grace of what radiated from the wonderful etheric body of Christian Rosenkreutz, they could develop an absolutely new world conception. What has been developed by the Rosicrucians up to our time is work of both an outer and an inner nature. The outer work was for the purpose of discovering what lies behind the illusion of the material world. They wanted to investigate the illusion of matter. Just as the human being has an etheric body, so does the whole of the macrocosm have an etheric macrocosm, an etheric body.

There is a certain point of transition from the coarser to the finer substance. Let us look at the boundary between physical and etheric substance. What lies between physical and etheric substance is like nothing else in the world. It is neither gold nor silver, lead nor copper. It is something that cannot be compared with any other physical substance, yet it is the essence of all of them. It is a substance that is contained in every other physical substance, so that the other physical substances can be considered to be modifications of this one substance. To see this substance clairvoyantly was the endeavour of the Rosicrucians. The preparation, the development of such vision they recognized as requiring a heightened activity of the soul's moral forces, which would then enable them to see this substance. They realized that the power for this vision lay in the moral power of the soul. This substance was really seen and discovered by the Rosicrucians. They found that this substance lived in the world in a certain form both in the macrocosm and in the human being. In the world outside the human being they revered it as the mighty garment of the macrocosm. They saw it arising in the human being when there is a harmonious interplay between thinking and the will. They saw the will forces as being not only in man but in the macrocosm also, for instance in thunder and lightning. And they saw the forces of thought on the one hand in human beings and also outside in the world, in the rainbow and the rosy light of dawn. The Rosicrucians sought the strength to achieve such harmony of will and thinking in their own soul, in the forces radiating from this etheric body of the thirteenth, Christian Rosenkreutz.

It was established that all the discoveries they made had to remain the secret of the Rosicrucians for a hundred years, and that not until a hundred years had passed might these Rosicrucian revelations be divulged to the world, for not until they had worked at them for a hundred years might they talk about them in an appropriate way. Thus what appeared in 1785 in the work *The Secret Symbols of the Rosicrucians* was being prepared from the seventeenth to the eighteenth century.

Now it is also of great importance to know that in any century the Rosicrucian inspiration is given in such a way that the name of the one who receives the inspiration is never made public. Only the highest initiates know it. Today, for instance, only those occurrences can be made public that happened a hundred years ago, for that is the time that must pass before it is permissible to speak of it in the outside world. The temptation fanatically to idealize a person bearing such authority would be too great, which is the worst thing that could happen. It would be too near to idolatry. This silence, however, is not only essential in order to avoid the outer temptations of ambition and pride, which could probably be overcome, but above all to avoid occult astral attacks which would be constantly directed at an individuality of that calibre. That is why it is an essential condition that a fact like this can only be spoken of after a hundred years. Through the works of the Rosicrucians, the etheric body of Christian Rosenkreutz became ever stronger and mightier from century to century. It worked not only through Christian Rosenkreutz but through all those who became his pupils. From the fourteenth century onwards, Christian Rosenkreutz has been incarnated again and again. Everything that is revealed in the name of anthroposophy is strengthened by the etheric body of Christian Rosenkreutz, and those who make anthroposophy known let themselves be overshadowed by this etheric body that can work on them both when Christian Rosenkreutz is incarnated and when he is not in incarnation.

The Count of Saint-Germain was the exoteric name of Christian Rosenkreutz's incarnation in the eighteenth century.[21] This name was given to other people, too, however; therefore not everything that is told about the Count of Saint-Germain in the outside world applies to the real Christian Rosenkreutz. Christian Rosenkreutz is incarnated again today. The inspiration for the work of H.P. Blavatsky, *Isis Unveiled*, came from the strength radiating from his etheric body. It was also Christian Rosenkreutz's influence working invisibly on Lessing that inspired him to write *The Education of the Human Race* (1780). Because of the rising tide of materialism, it became more and more difficult for inspiration to come about in the Rosicrucian way. Then in the nineteenth century came the high tide of materialism. Many things could only be made available in a very incomplete way. In 1851, the problem of the immortality of the soul was resolved by Widenmann through the idea of reincarnation. His text was awarded a prize. Around 1850 Drossbach wrote from a psychological point of view in support of reincarnation.

Thus the forces radiating from the etheric body of Christian Rosenkreutz continued to be active in the nineteenth century too. And a renewal of theosophical life could come about because by 1899 the short Kali Yuga had run its course. That is why it is now easier to approach the spiritual world and why a far greater degree of spiritual influence is possible. The etheric body of Christian Rosenkreutz has become very powerful and, through devotion to it, human beings will be able to acquire new clairvoyance and invoke lofty spiritual forces. This will only be possible, however, for those people who follow the training of Christian Rosenkreutz correctly. Until now, an esoteric Rosicrucian preparation was essential, but the twentieth century has the mission of enabling this etheric body to become so mighty that it can also work exoterically.

Those affected by it will be granted an experience of the event that Paul experienced on the road to Damascus. Until now, this etheric body has only worked upon the Rosicrucian school; in the twentieth century more and more people will be able to experience the effect of it, and through this they will come to experience the appearance of Christ in the etheric body.[22] It is the work of the Rosicrucians that makes possible etheric vision of Christ. The number of people who will become capable of seeing it will grow and grow. We must attribute this reappearance to the important work of the twelve and the thirteenth in the thirteenth and fourteenth centuries.

If you manage to become an instrument of Christian Rosenkreutz, then you can be assured that the tiniest details of your soul-life will be there for eternity.

2. The Working of Christian Rosenkreutz — Then and Today

Meeting Christian Rosenkreutz as one's teacher is not simply an event like any other, nor is it a matter of receiving teaching in an external way. Rudolf Steiner helps us become prepared to recognize the moments when the Rosicrucian 'calling' takes place, and to be ready inwardly to respond. This requires us to achieve our own inner freedom, and to be able to recognize the validity of different, complementary points of view — for it is only through individuals, in freedom, that Rosicrucian wisdom can work.

A kind of intuitive perception of these events has arisen in people who know something of the history of spiritual life. Goethe's poem *The Mysteries* has been recited for us many times. Goethe speaks in that poem of the council of the twelve on the basis of a deep, intuitive perception, and he has been able to convey to us the mood of heart and feeling in which they lived. The thirteenth was not brother Mark[23] but the child of whom I have been telling you, and who almost immediately after his birth was taken into the care of the twelve and was brought up by them until the age of manhood. The child developed in a strange and remarkable way. The twelve were not in any sense fanatics; they were of inner composure, enlightenment and peace of heart. How do fanatics behave? They want to convert people as quickly as possible, while they, as a rule, do not want to be converted. Everybody is expected immediately to believe what the fanatics want them to believe and they are angry when this does not happen. In our day, when someone sets out to expound a particular subject, people simply do not believe that his aim may be not to voice his own views but something quite different, that is, the thoughts and opinions of the one of whom he is writing. For many years I was held to be a follower of Nietzsche because I once wrote an absolutely objective book about him. People simply cannot understand that the aim of a writer may be to give an objective exposition. They think that everyone must be fanatically promoting his own view of the subject of which he happens to be speaking.

The twelve in the thirteenth century were far from being fanatics, and they were very sparing with oral teaching. But simply by living in communion with the boy, twelve rays of light, as we might describe it, went out from them into him and were resolved in his soul into one great harmony. It would not have been possible to give him any kind of academic examination; nevertheless there lived within him, transmuted into feeling and sensitive perception, all that the twelve representatives of the twelve different types of religion poured into his soul. His whole soul reflected the harmony of the twelve different forms of belief spread over the earth.

In this way the soul of the boy had to bear a great deal, and consequently it worked in a strange way upon the body. And it is precisely for this reason that the process of which I am telling you now cannot be repeated; it could only be enacted at that particular time.

Strange to say, as the harmony within the boy's soul increased, his body became more delicate—more and more delicate, until at a certain age it was transparent in every limb. The boy ate less and less until he finally took no nourishment at all. Then he lay for days in a condition of complete torpor; the soul had left the body, and returned into it again after a few days. The youth was now inwardly quite changed. The twelve different rays of human outlook were united in one single radiance, and he gave utterance to the greatest, most wonderful secrets. He did not repeat what the first, or the second, or the third had said, but spoke in a new and wonderful synthesis all that they would have said had they spoken in unison; all the knowledge they possessed was gathered into one whole, and when he uttered it, it was as though this new wisdom had just come to birth in him. It was as though a higher spirit were speaking in him. Something entirely and essentially new was thus imparted to the twelve wise men. Wisdom in abundance was imparted to them, and to each, individually, greater illumination concerning what he had hitherto known. I have been describing to you the first school of Christian Rosenkreutz, for the thirteenth is the individuality known to us by that name. In that incarnation he died after only a brief earthly existence; in the fourteenth century he was born again and lived then for more than a hundred years. All those things again appeared in him that had developed in him in the thirteenth century. Then his life had been brief, but in the fourteenth century it was very long. During the first half of this later incarnation he went on great journeys in search of the different centres of culture in Europe, Africa and Asia, in order to gather knowledge of what had come to life in him during the previous century. Then he returned to Europe. A few of those who had brought him up in the thirteenth century were again in incarnation and were joined by others. This was the time of the inauguration of the Rosicrucian stream of spiritual life. And Christian Rosenkreutz himself incarnated again and again.

To this very day he is at work — including during the brief intervals when he is not actually in incarnation; through his higher bodies he then works spiritually into human beings, without the need of physical contact. We must try to picture the mysterious way in which his influence operates.

And I want to begin here by giving an example. Those who participate consciously in the occult life of the spirit had a strange experience from the 'eighties on into the 'nineties of the nineteenth century; they became aware of certain influences emanating from a remarkable personality (I am only mentioning one case among many). There was, however, something not quite harmonious about those influences. Anyone who is sensitive to influences from contemporaries living a great distance away would at that time have been aware of something raying out from a certain personality, which was not altogether harmonious. When the new century dawned, however, these influences became harmonious. What had happened? I will tell you the reason for this. On 12 August 1900 Soloviev died — a man far too little appreciated or understood.[24] The influences of his etheric body radiated far and wide, but although Soloviev was a great philosopher, in his case the development of his soul was in advance of that of his head, his intellect; he was a great and splendid thinker, but his conscious philosophy was of far less significance than that which he bore in his soul. Up to the time of his death the head was a hindering factor and so, as an occult influence, he had an inharmonious effect. But once he died and the etheric body, separated from the brain, rayed out in the etheric world, he was liberated from the restrictions caused by his thinking, and the rays of his influence shone out with wonderful brilliance and power.

People may ask: how can such knowledge really be of relevance to us? This question in itself is an illusion, for the human being is shaped on every level by the spiritual processes around him; and when certain esotericists become aware of the reality of these processes, it is because they actually see them. But spiritual processes operate too in those others who do not see. Everything in the spiritual world is interconnected. Whatever influence may radiate from a highly developed Frenchman or Russian is felt not only on their own native soil, but their thought and influence has an effect over the whole earth. Everything that happens in the spiritual world has an influence on us, and only when we realize that the soul lives in the spiritual world just as the lung does within the air shall we have the right attitude.

The forces in the etheric bodies of highly developed individualities stream out and have a potent effect upon other human beings. So, too, the etheric body of Christian Rosenkreutz works far and wide in the world. And reference must be made here to a fact that is of the greatest significance to many people; it is something that transpires in the spiritual world between death and a new birth and is not to be ascribed to chance.

Christian Rosenkreutz has always made use of the short intervals of time between his incarnations to call into his particular stream of spiritual life those souls whom he knows to be ready; between his deaths and births he concerns himself with choosing those who are ready to enter his stream. But human beings themselves, by learning to be attentive, must be able to recognize by what means Christian Rosenkreutz gives them a sign showing them that they may count themselves among his chosen. This sign has been given in the lives of very many human beings of the present time, but they pay no heed to it. Yet among the apparently chance happenings in a person's life, there is for many people one in particular that is to be regarded as an indication that between death and a new birth Christian Rosenkreutz found him mature and ready; the sign is given by Christian Rosenkreutz on the physical plane, however. This event may be called the mark of Christian Rosenkreutz. Let us suppose someone is lying in bed – in other places I have mentioned different kinds of occurrence, but all of them have happened – and for some unaccountable reason he suddenly wakes up and, as though guided by instinct, looks at a wall that is usually quite dark. The room is dimly lit, the wall is dark, when suddenly he sees written on the wall: 'Get up at once!' It all seems very strange, but he gets up and leaves the house, and hardly has he done so when the ceiling over his bed collapses; although nobody else would have been in danger of getting hurt, he himself would inevitably have been killed. The most thorough investigation proves that nobody on the physical plane warned him to get up. If he had remained lying there he would certainly have been killed.

Such an experience may be thought to be a hallucination or something of the kind, but deeper investigation will reveal that these particular experiences—and they come to hundreds of people—are not accidental. A beckoning call has come from Christian Rosenkreutz. The karma of the one called in this way always indicates that Christian Rosenkreutz bestows the life he may claim. I say explicitly: such occurrences occur in the lives of many people at the present time, and it is only a question of being awake to them. The occurrence does not always take such a dramatic form as the example quoted, but numbers of human beings nowadays have had such experiences. Now when I say something more than once during a lecture, I do so quite deliberately, because I find that strange conclusions are apt to be drawn from things that are half or totally forgotten. I say this because nobody need be discouraged who has had no such experience; this might not be the case, for if he searches he will certainly find something of the kind in his life. Naturally I can only single out a typical example. Here, then, we have in our life a fact of which we may say that its cause does not lie in the period of actual incarnation; we may have met

Christian Rosenkreutz in the spiritual world. I have laid particular stress on this exceptional event of the call. Other events, too, could be mentioned, events connected directly with the spiritual world that occur during the life between death and a new birth; but in our spiritual context this particular event should be of special significance for us as it is so intimately connected with our spiritual movement.

Such an event surely indicates that we must develop a quite different attitude if we want to have a clear vision of what influences actually affect our lives. Most human beings rush hectically through life and are not thoughtful and attentive; many people say that one should not brood but engage in a life of action. But how much better it would be if precipitate actions were left undone and people were to reflect a little – their deeds would then be far more mature! If only the beckoning call were heeded with composure and attentiveness. Often it only seems as if we are dreaming or brooding, but it is precisely through quiet composure that strength comes to us – and then we shall follow when karma calls and understand its call. These are the things I wanted to call your attention to today, for they do indeed make life more comprehensible.

* * *

I should say, of course, that this is only the external sign of being outwardly qualified for a spiritual calling. To be inwardly qualified, the chosen person has to have an interest in something spiritual, anthroposophy or some other form of spiritual science. The external event I have described is a fact of the physical world, though it does not come by means of a human voice. The event always occurs in such a way that the person concerned knows quite clearly that the voice comes from the spiritual world. He may at first imagine that the voice has come from a human being who is hidden somewhere, but when the pupil is mature enough he discovers that it was not a physical person intervening in his life. In short, this event convinces the pupil that there are messages from the spiritual world. Such events can occur once or many times in life. We have to understand what effect this has on the soul of the pupil. The pupil tells himself: 'I have received another life through grace; the first one was forfeited.' This new life given him through grace sheds light on the whole of the pupil's further life. He has a definite feeling which can be described in this way: without this Rosicrucian experience of mine I should have died; my subsequent life would not have had the same value but for this event.

It can happen, of course, that even though someone has already experienced this once or even several times he does not immediately come to anthroposophy or spiritual science. Later on, however, the memory of the event can come back. Many of you here can examine the past course of your lives and you will find that similar occurrences have happened to you. We give too little attention to such things today. We ought to realize how very important occurrences pass by without us noticing them. This is an indication of the way the more advanced pupils of Rosicrucianism are summoned.

This kind of occurrence will either pass a person by without being noticed at all, in which case the impression is blotted out and he attaches no importance to it, or, assuming the person to be attentive, he will appreciate its significance and he will then perhaps realize that he was actually facing a crisis then, a karmic crisis; his life should actually have ended at that moment. He had forfeited his life, and was only saved by something resembling chance. Since that hour a second life has been grafted on to the first, as it were. You must look on this life as a gift and live it accordingly.

When such an event awakens in a person, the inner sense of looking at one's life from that time onwards as a gift makes such a person nowadays a follower of Christian Rosenkreutz. For that is his way of calling these souls to him. And whoever can recall having had such an experience can tell himself: 'Christian Rosenkreutz has given me a sign from the spiritual world that I belong to his stream. Christian Rosenkreutz has added the possibility of such an experience to my karma.' That is the way in which Christian Rosenkreutz makes his choice of pupils. He chooses his community like this. Whoever experiences this consciously, knows: 'A path has been shown me, and I must follow it and see how far I can use my powers to serve Rosicrucianism.' Those who have not understood the sign, however, will do so at a later time, for whoever has received the sign will not be free of it again.

That a person can have an experience of the kind described is due to his having met Christian Rosenkreutz in the spiritual world between his last death and his latest birth. Christian Rosenkreutz chose us then, and he put an impulse of will into us that now leads us to such experiences. This is the way in which spiritual connections are brought about.

3. Christian Rosenkreutz as the Guardian of Modern Knowledge

The phase of natural science and the 'onlooker' consciousness has its rightful place in humanity's inner development, as well as giving us mastery over the external world. Nevertheless, we need for the future to move forward into a spiritual-scientific epoch. Rosicrucianism does not reject natural science; indeed Rudolf Steiner shows how it helped bring natural science into being, just as it now demands that we develop new ways of thinking so as to begin understanding the inner dimension. In the wonderful parable and deeply esoteric work The Chymical Wedding of Christian Rosenkreutz *it is narrated how as the great initiate of modern times he takes place at the 'threshold', where new ideas and forms are created out of the spirit so as to flow into future life.*

From ancient to modern in Rosicrucian teachings

To go further, let us discuss the difference between Christian Rosenkreutz's teaching in earlier times and in later times. This teaching used to be more in the nature of natural science, whereas today it is more like spiritual science. In earlier times, for instance, people observed natural processes and called this science alchemy;[25] and when such processes took place beyond the earth they called it astrology. Today we start from a more spiritual perspective. If we consider, for instance, the successive post-Atlantean cultural epochs, the culture of ancient India, ancient Iran, the Egyptian-Mesopotamian-Assyrian-Babylonian culture and the Graeco-Roman culture, we learn about the nature of the development of the human soul. The Rosicrucians of the Middle Ages studied natural processes, regarding them as the earth processes of nature. They distinguished, for instance, three different natural processes which they regarded as the three great processes of nature.

The first important process is the salt process. Everything in nature that can form a deposit of hard substance out of a solution was called salt by the medieval Rosicrucians. When the medieval Rosicrucians saw this salt formation, however, their conception of it was entirely different from that of a modern person. For if they wanted to feel they had understood it, the witnessing of such a process had to work like a prayer in their souls. Therefore the medieval Rosicrucians tried to make clear to themselves what would have to happen in their own soul if the formation of salt were to take place there too. They arrived at the thought: 'Human nature is perpetually destroying itself through instincts and passions. Our life would be nothing but decomposition, a process of putrefaction, if we only followed our instincts and passions. And if human beings really want to protect themselves against this process of putrefaction, then they must constantly devote themselves to noble thoughts that turn them towards the spirit.' It was a matter of bringing their thoughts to a higher level of development.

The medieval Rosicrucians knew that if they did not combat their passions in one incarnation they would be born with a predisposition for illness in the next one, but that if they purified their passion they would enter life in the next incarnation with a predisposition for health. The process of overcoming, through spirituality, the forces that lead to decay is microcosmic salt formation. So we can understand how a natural process like this occasioned the most reverent prayer. When observing salt formation, the medieval Rosicrucians told themselves with a feeling of deepest piety: 'Divine spiritual powers have been working in this process for thousands of years in the same way as noble thoughts work in me. I am praying to the thoughts of the gods, the thoughts of divine spiritual beings that are behind the *maya* [illusion] of nature.' The medieval Rosicrucians knew this, and they said to themselves: 'When I let nature stimulate me to develop feelings like this, I make myself like the macrocosm. If I observe this process in an external way only, I cut myself off from the gods, I fall away from the macrocosm.' Such were the feelings of the medieval theosophists or Rosicrucians.

The process of dissolution gave a different experience; it was a different natural process that could also lead the medieval Rosicrucians to prayer. Everything that can dissolve something else was called by the medieval Rosicrucians quicksilver or mercury. Now they asked again: 'What is the corresponding quality in the human soul? What quality works in the soul in the same way in which quicksilver or mercury works outside in nature?' The medieval

Love → Mercury

Rosicrucians knew that all the forms of love in the soul are what correspond to mercury. They distinguished between lower and higher processes of dissolution, just as there are lower and higher forms of love. And thus the witnessing of the dissolution process again became a pious prayer, and the medieval theosophists said to themselves: 'God's love has been at work out there for thousands of years in the same way as love works in me.'

The third important natural process for the medieval theosophists was combustion that takes place when material substance is consumed by flames. And again the medieval Rosicrucians sought the inner process corresponding to this combustion. They saw this inner soul process to be ardent devotion to the Deity. And everything that can go up in flames they called sulphur. In the stages of development of the earth they beheld a gradual process of purification similar to a combustion or sulphur process. Just as they knew that the earth will at some time be purified by fire, they also saw a combustion process in fervent devotion to the Deity. In the earth processes they beheld the work of those gods who look up to mightier gods above them. And permeated with great piety and deeply religious feelings at the spectacle of the process of combustion, they told themselves: 'Gods are now making a sacrifice to higher gods.' And then when the medieval theosophists produced the combustion process in the laboratory themselves, they felt: 'I am doing the same as the gods do when they sacrifice themselves to higher gods.' They only considered themselves worthy to carry out such a process of combustion in their laboratory when they felt themselves filled with the mood of sacrifice, when they themselves were filled with the desire to devote themselves in sacrifice to the gods. The power of the flame filled the medieval theosophists with lofty and deeply religious feelings, and they told themselves: 'When I see flames outside in the macrocosm I am seeing the thoughts and the love of the gods, and the gods' willingness to sacrifice, to make offerings.'

A medieval Rosicrucian produced these processes in his laboratory and then he entered into contemplation of these salt formations, solutions and processes of combustion, letting himself at the same time be filled with deeply religious feelings in which he became aware of his connection with all the forces of the macrocosm. These soul processes called forth in him divine thoughts, divine love and divine sacrifice. And then the medieval Rosicrucian discovered that when he produced a salt process, noble, purifying thoughts arose in him. With a solution process love was stimulated in him, he was inspired by divine love; and with a combustion process the desire to make a sacrifice was kindled in him, it urged him to sacrifice himself on the altar of the world.

These were the experiences of a person who did these experiments. And if you had attended these experiments yourself in clairvoyant vision, you would have perceived a change in the aura of the person carrying them out. The aura that was a mixture of colours before the experiment began, being full of instincts and desires to which the person in question had perhaps succumbed, became single-hued as a result of the experiment. First of all, during the experiment with salt formation, it became the colour of copper — pure, divine thoughts; then, in the experiment with a solution, the colour of silver — divine love; and finally, with combustion, the colour of gold — divine sacrifice. And then the alchemists said they had made subjective copper, subjective silver and subjective gold out of the aura. And the outcome was that the person who had undergone this, and had really experienced such an experiment inwardly, was completely permeated by divine love. Such was the way these medieval theosophists became permeated with purity, love and the will to sacrifice, and by means of this sacrificial service they prepared themselves for a certain clairvoyance. This is how the medieval theosophists could see behind *maya* into the way spiritual beings helped things to come into being and pass away again. And this enabled them to realize which forces of aspiration in our souls are helpful and which are not. They became acquainted with our own forces of growth and decay. The medieval theosophist Heinrich Khunrath,[26] in a moment of enlightenment, called this process the law of growth and decay. Through observing nature, the medieval theosophists learnt the law of ascending and descending evolution. The science they acquired from this they expressed in certain signs, imaginative pictures and figures. It was a kind of imaginative knowledge. One of the outcomes of this was *The Secret Symbols of the Rosicrucians* mentioned previously.

This is the way the best alchemists worked from the fourteenth to the eighteenth and until the beginning of the nineteenth century. Nothing has been published about this truly moral, ethical, intellectual work. What has been written about alchemy concerns purely external experiments only, and was only written by those who performed alchemy as an end in itself. The false alchemist wanted to create physical substance. When he experimented with the burning of substances he saw the material results as the only thing gained, whereas the genuine alchemist attached no importance to these material results. For him it all depended on the inner soul experiences he had whilst the substance was forming, the thoughts and experiences within him. Therefore there was a strict rule that the medieval theosophist who produced gold and silver from his experiments was never allowed to profit from it himself. He was only allowed to give away the metals thus produced. People today no longer have the correct conception of these experiments. We have no idea what the person conducting the experiment could experience. The medieval theosophist was able to experience whole dramas of the soul in his laboratory when, for example, antimony was extracted; the people conducting these experiments saw significant moral forces at work in these processes.

If these things had not taken place at that time, we would not be able to practise Rosicrucianism on the basis of spiritual science today. What the medieval Rosicrucian experienced when he beheld the processes of nature was a holy science. The mood of spiritual sacrifice, the tremendous joys, the great natural events, the pain and sadness too, as well as the events that uplifted him and made him happy, all these experiences that he had during the experiment he performed worked on him in a liberating and redeeming way. All that was planted in him then, however, is now hidden in the innermost depths of the human being.

How shall we rediscover these hidden forces that used to lead to clairvoyance? We shall find them by studying spiritual science and by devoting ourselves deeply to the soul's inner life in serious meditation and concentration. By means of inner development of this kind, work with nature will gradually become a sacrificial rite again. For this to come about, human beings must go through what we now call spiritual science. Human beings in their thousands must devote themselves to the science of the spirit; they must cultivate an inner life, so that in the future the spiritual reality behind nature will be perceptible again, and we will learn to understand again the spirit behind *maya*. Then, in the future, although it will only happen to small numbers to begin with, people will be able to experience Paul's vision on the road to Damascus and to perceive the etheric Christ, who will come among us in supersensory form. But before this happens, man will have to return to a spiritual view of nature. If we were not aware of the full significance of Rosicrucianism, we could believe that humanity was still at the same stage as it was two thousand years ago. Until human beings have gone through this process, which is only possible by means of spiritual science, they will not achieve spiritual vision. There are many good and pious people who are theosophists at heart, although they are not followers of spiritual science.

Through the event of the baptism in the Jordan, when the

Christ descended into the body of Jesus of Nazareth, and through the Mystery of Golgotha, mankind became capable of later beholding and recognizing the Christ in the etheric body—in our century in fact, from 1930 onwards. Christ has only walked the earth once in a physical body, and we should learn to understand this. 'The second coming of Christ' means seeing Christ supersensibly in the etheric. Therefore everyone who wants to tread the right path of development must work to acquire the capacity to see with spiritual eyes. It would not signify human progress for Christ to appear again in a physical body. His next appearance will be a revelation in the etheric body.

What was given in the different religious creeds has been gathered into one whole by Christian Rosenkreutz and the council of the twelve. This means that everything that the separate religions had to give and all that their followers strove and longed for will be found in the Christ impulse. Development during the next three thousand years will consist in the establishment and furthering of an understanding of the Christ impulse. From the twentieth century onwards all religions will come to be reconciled in the mystery of Rosicrucianism. And in the course of the next three thousand years this will become possible because it will no longer be necessary to teach from records or documents; for through beholding Christ, human beings will themselves learn to understand the experience Paul had on the way to Damascus. Humankind itself will pass through the experience of Paul.

Christian Rosenkreutz at the 'Chymical Wedding'

The further development of nature-related alchemy forms the work of the fifth day of *The Chymical Wedding of Christian Rosenkreutz* by Johann Valentin Andreae.[27] There it is described how the vision of the seeker for the spirit must penetrate into the processes produced by nature when it brings forth growing life. And he must transform this creative activity of nature into the forces of knowledge without allowing death to prevail in the transition from growth to soul processes. He receives the forces of knowledge from nature as dead entities which he has to animate by restoring everything of which nature deprived them when it brought about their alchemical transmutation into powers of cognition. As he moves towards this goal, a temptation approaches him. He must descend into the region where through the force of love, nature charms life from what inherently is striving towards death. Here he is in danger of his vision being seized upon by those instincts that prevail in the lower regions of substances. He has to learn to recognize how in matter, which bears the stamp of death, lives an element related to the love underlying every renewal of life.

This exposure of the soul to temptation is very significantly described by Andreae when he makes Christian Rosenkreutz appear before Venus while Cupid is playing his role. And it is clearly indicated how the seeker for the spirit here referred to is not restrained by such temptation from pursuing his onward course by his own soul forces alone as well as by the working of other powers. If Christian

Rosenkreutz had to tread only his own path of knowledge, the latter could have ended in temptation. The fact that this is not the case indicates what Andreae wishes to portray. On his spiritual path, Christian Rosenkreutz is meant to show the way from a past epoch to the dawn of another.

The active powers of the ages help him to permeate his ego with the powers of knowledge appropriate for the new period. Hence he can proceed on his journey to the 'Tower' by participating in the alchemical process through which the dead powers of cognition experience their resurrection. Also on this journey, this now gives him the power of listening to the Siren's love song without falling victim to its seductions. The fundamental spiritual force of love must work upon him, but he must not allow the way that it manifests itself in the sensory world to mislead him on his way. In the Tower of Olympus the dead forces of cognition are penetrated with the impulses which in the ordinary human organism are active only in the growth processes. It is shown how Christian Rosenkreutz is allowed to take part in this event because his soul development is to proceed in accordance with the changing forces of the ages. Instead of going to sleep, he goes into the garden, looks up at the starry heavens and observes to himself: 'Because I have this good opportunity to reflect on astronomy, I found that on this night a conjunction of planets takes place which is not often to be seen.'

In the experiences of the sixth day, we have a detailed description of the various imaginations that make clear in Christian Rosenkreutz's soul how the dead forces of cognition evolved by the organism in its ordinary journey through life are transmuted into supersensory powers of perception. Each of these imaginations corresponds to an experience of the soul in relation to its own powers when it realizes how what until now could be permeated only by death becomes capable of consciously allowing the living to stir within it. The individual pictures would be differently described by seekers for the spirit other than Andreae. But it is not a question of the content of single pictures but of the transformation of a person's soul forces through having before him in a succession of imaginations such pictures as reflections of this transformation. Christian Rosenkreutz is portrayed in *The Chymical Wedding* as the seeker for the spirit who feels the approach of that period when humanity will view nature's phenomena differently from the epoch passing away with the fifteenth century.

In this coming period, as they observe nature, human beings will no longer be able to perceive the spiritual content of the objects and events of nature through such observation alone. This can lead to a denial of the spiritual world if human beings do not admit the existence of a path of knowledge by which the material basis of the soul life can be penetrated while the spirit is received into this knowledge. To be able to achieve this, we must be able to shed spiritual light upon the material basis. We must be able to perceive how nature proceeds as it shapes its active forces into a soul organism through which death is revealed; then we can learn from the being of nature itself the mystery of how spirit can confront spirit when the creative activity of nature is guided to awaking the dead forces of cognition to a higher life. In this way knowledge develops which, as spirit-knowledge, finds its place in reality. For knowledge of this kind is a further outgrowth on the living being of the world; through it is continued the evolution of reality from the first primeval beginnings of existence up to human life. By this means alone is developed into higher forces of knowledge what already exists in nature as a germ, but which is held back from working in nature itself at the point where, in the metamorphosis of existence, the cognition of what is dead should be developed. The objection that such a continuation of nature's activity beyond what is attained by it in the human organism would lead beyond reality and into the unreal will not be made by anyone who penetrates into the evolution of nature itself. For everywhere evolution consists in the progress of the forces of growth being arrested at a certain point in order to bring about revelations of the endless possibilities of new forms at further stages of human existence.

Thus the human organization also contains the possibility of being held back in its development. But just as development is arrested in the green leaf of the plant, and yet the formative forces of the plant's growth advance beyond this form, making the coloured leaf of the blossom appear at a higher stage, so the human being can progress from the formation of his forces of knowledge, which are directed towards what is dead, to a higher stage of these forces. He experiences the reality of this progress by becoming aware that through it he receives the soul organ for the comprehension of the supersensory revelation of the spirit, just as the transformation of the green leaf into the coloured flower organ of the plant prepares the capacity that expands itself into the formation of the fruit.

After the alchemical process in art is completed, Christian Rosenkreutz is named 'Knight of the Golden Stone'. One would have to enter deeply into a purely historical description if one wished to elaborate on the name 'Golden Stone' from the literature — some trustworthy but, for the greater part, fraudulent — to show how it was used. But that is not the purpose of this article. However, we can simply indicate the conclusions concerning the use of the name drawn from such literature. The individuals who can be taken seriously who have used the name 'The Golden Stone' wanted to indicate by it that it is possible to understand the dead nature of stones in its relationship to what is living and what is coming to life. The serious alchemist believed it would be possible for artificial processes of nature to be produced using material of a dead and stony character, making it possible to recognize something, when rightly observed, of what goes on when nature itself weaves the dead into what is alive and developing. Through the perception of quite distinct processes in what is dead, traces of the creative activity of nature and with it the essence of the spirit ruling in the phenomena would be understood.

The symbol for the dead element that is recognized as the revelation of the spirit is 'The Golden Stone'. Whoever examines a corpse in its essential, true nature recognizes how what is dead is gathered up within the general processes of nature. It is the form of the corpse, however, which opposes this general process of nature. This form can only be a result of spirit-permeated life. The general processes of nature must destroy what has been formed by spirit-permeated life. The alchemist is of the opinion that what ordinary human knowledge can grasp of the whole of nature is only as much as what of the human being can be identified by his corpse. A higher knowledge should find in natural phenomena what is related to such knowledge in the same way as the spirit-permeated life is related to the corpse. Such is the striving for 'The Golden Stone'.

Andreae speaks of this symbol in such a way as to indicate clearly that only those can understand what to do with 'The Golden Stone' who have experienced what he describes as the six days' work. He wishes to show that anyone who has spoken of this without knowing the nature of the transformation of the forces of cognition can have only an illusion in mind. In Christian Rosenkreutz he strives to describe a personality who can speak in an authoritative way about something often spoken of without authority. He wishes to defend the truth against what is wrongly spoken about the search for the spiritual world.

After they have become actual workers on 'The Golden Stone', Christian Rosenkreutz and his companions receive a memento with the two sayings 'Art is the servant of nature' and 'Nature is the daughter of time'. Out of their spiritual knowledge they are to work in harmony with these guiding tenets. They comprise and characterize the six days' experiences. Nature reveals its mysteries to him who through his art enables himself to continue its creative work.

But in this continuation he cannot succeed unless in his art he has first listened to the meaning of nature's will, and unless he has recognized how nature's revelations arise through its infinite faculty of evolution, emerging from the womb of time in finite forms of existence.

In this connection, we are shown with the king on the seventh day how Christian Rosenkreutz as seeker for the spirit now stands in relation to his transformed faculties of knowledge. We are shown how as 'father' he himself gave birth to them. And his relation to the 'first gatekeeper' is a relation to a part of his own being—to what as 'Astrologus' searched for the laws determining human life before the transformation of his forces of cognition. But at that time his being was not equal to facing the temptation resulting when the seeker for the spirit encounters a situation like that in which Christian Rosenkreutz was placed at the beginning of the fifth day upon confronting Venus. Anyone who succumbs to this temptation does not find entry to the spiritual world. He knows too much to be entirely shut away from it, but he cannot enter. He has to stand guard before the door until another appears and falls victim to the same temptation. Christian Rosenkreutz supposes himself to have succumbed and thus to have been condemned to take over the office of guardian. But this guardian is part of himself, and because he can observe it with the other transformed part of himself he is able to overcome it. He becomes guardian of his own soul life, but this guardianship does not hinder him from establishing a free connection with the spiritual world. Through his seven days' experience, Christian Rosenkreutz has become a person knowledgeable in the spirit who with the power conferred on him by this experience can work in the world.

What Christian Rosenkreutz and his associates accomplish in external life flows from the spirit out of which the works of nature themselves flow. Through their work they bring into human life a harmony which is an image of the harmony working in nature, capable of conquering opposing inharmonies. The presence of such people in society is a continuously active impulse towards a health-sustaining way of life. When people ask what are the best laws for living together, for the social life of human beings on earth, Andreae points to Christian Rosenkreutz and his companions. He answers: the social order cannot be regulated by ideas expressed in thoughts as to how this or that shall be done, but by what may be said by those who strive to live in the spirit manifesting itself through what is. What guides the souls who, in the spirit of Christian Rosenkreutz, wish to work in human life is expressed in five points.

It is far from them to think out of any spirit other than the one revealing itself in the creations of nature; and they see the work of human beings as a continuation of nature's works.

They do not place their work in the service of human impulses, but make these impulses into mediators for the works of the spirit.

They serve human beings lovingly, so that in the relation between person and person the creative spirit can be manifested.

They are not to let themselves be led by anything of worth the world could give, aside from their striving for the worth the spirit can confer upon all human labour.

They are not, like bad alchemists, to fall into the error of confusing the physical with the spiritual. Bad alchemists think that the physical means of prolonging life or similar objectives are of the highest value, forgetting that the physical is of value only so long as its existence is a rightful manifestation of the underlying spirit.[28]

At the end of the narrative of *The Chymical Wedding*, Andreae describes Christian Rosenkreutz's homecoming. In all external respects he is the same as he was before his experiences. The new situation of his life is different from the old only in so far as from that time on he will carry his 'higher human being' within himself as the ruler of his consciousness, and what he accomplishes will be what the 'higher human being' can effect through him. The transition from the last experiences of the seventh day to finding himself at home in his ordinary surroundings is not described. 'Here two or three pages are missing.' One could imagine there might be people who would be especially curious about what these missing pages contain. This latter is what only he can know who himself has undergone an individual experience of the transformation of his soul-nature. Such a person knows that everything leading to this experience has a universally human significance which is communicated as one communicates the experience of a journey. The reception of what has been experienced by the ordinary person is, on the contrary, something quite personal; it is different for each one and cannot be understood by another in the same way as by the one who has experienced it. That Johann Valentin Andreae has not described this transition into the ordinary circumstances of life serves as further proof that *The Chymical Wedding* expresses true knowledge of what had to be described.

4. The Cosmic Mission of Christian Rosenkreutz

Since Christian Rosenkreutz works not only from the physical but from the spiritual world, he is able to help humanity in the spheres beyond death – in turn affecting their destiny in future incarnations on earth. This work has indeed become specially necessary since humanity entered the dark phase of materialistic thought. Rudolf Steiner's account not only gives us a glimpse of that cosmic mission but shows how it reveals the deep esoteric connections between world religions such as Buddhism and Christianity.

Anyone who, like Christian Rosenkreutz, appears in the world as a leading esotericist has to reckon with the conditions peculiar to his epoch. The intrinsic nature of modern culture developed for the first time when the new natural science arrived on the scene with Copernicus, Giordano Bruno, Galileo and others. Nowadays people are taught about Copernicus in their early schooldays, and the impressions thus received remain with them their whole life long. In earlier times the soul experienced something different. Try to picture to yourselves what a contrast there is between a person of the modern age and one who lived centuries ago. Before the days of Copernicus, everyone believed that the earth remained at rest in cosmic space with the sun and the stars revolving around it. The very ground slipped from under people's feet when Copernicus proposed the doctrine that the earth moves with tremendous speed through the universe. We should not underestimate the effects of such a revolution in thinking, accompanied as it was by a corresponding change in people's life of feeling. All thoughts and ideas were suddenly altered from what they had been before the days of Copernicus. And now let us ask: what does esotericism have to say about this revolution in thinking?

Anyone who brings an esoteric perspective to bear on the kind of world conception derived from Copernican tenets will have to admit that although these ideas can lead to great achievements in the realm of natural science and in outer life, they are incapable of promoting any understanding of the spiritual foundations of the world and the things of the world; there has never been a worse instrument for understanding the spiritual foundations of the world than the ideas of Copernicus—never in the whole of human evolution. The reason for this is that all these Copernican concepts are inspired by Lucifer.[29] Copernicanism is one of the last attacks, one of the last great attacks made by Lucifer upon the evolution of man. In earlier, pre-Copernican thought, the external world was indeed *maya*, but much traditional wisdom, much truth concerning the world and the things of the world still survived. Since Copernicus, however, man has *maya* around him not only in his material perceptions but in his very concepts and ideas. People take it for granted nowadays that the sun is firmly fixed in the centre and the planets revolve around it in ellipses. In the near future, however, it will be realized that the view of the world of the stars held by Copernicus is much less correct than the earlier Ptolemaic view. The view of the world held by the school of Copernicus and Kepler is very convenient, but as an explanation of the macrocosm it is not the truth.

And so Christian Rosenkreutz, confronted by a world conception which is itself a *maya*, an illusion, had to come to grips with it. Christian Rosenkreutz had to save esotericism in an age when all the concepts of science were themselves *maya*. In the middle of the sixteenth century, Copernicus' book *On the Revolutions of the Heavenly Spheres* appeared. At the end of the sixteenth century, the Rosicrucians were faced with the need to apply esotericism to understanding the planetary system, for with its materially conceived globes in space the Copernican planetary system was *maya*, even as a concept. Thus towards the end of the sixteenth century one of those conferences took place of which we heard here previously in connection with the initiation of Christian Rosenkreutz himself in the thirteenth century. This occult conference of leading individualities united Christian Rosenkreutz with the twelve individualities of that earlier time and certain other great leaders of humanity. There were present not only individuals in incarnation on the physical plane but also some who were in the spiritual worlds; and the individuality who in the sixth century before Christ had been incarnated as Gautama Buddha also participated.

The occultists of the East rightly believe—for they know it to be the truth—that the Buddha who in his twenty-ninth year rose from the rank of bodhisattva to become Buddha, had incarnated for the last time in a physical body. It is absolutely true that when the individuality of a bodhisattva becomes a Buddha he no longer appears on the earth in physical incarnation. But this does not mean that he ceases to be active in the affairs of the earth. The Buddha continues to work for the earth, although he is never again present in a physical body but sends down his influence from the spiritual world. The *Gloria* heard by the shepherds in the fields was an intimation from the spiritual world that the forces of Buddha were streaming into the astral body of the child Jesus described in St Luke's Gospel. The words of the *Gloria* came from Buddha who was working in the astral body of the child Jesus.[30] This wonderful message of peace and love is an integral part of Buddha's contribution to Christianity. But later on too, Buddha influenced the deeds of human beings — not physically but from the spiritual world — and he has co-operated in measures that have been necessary for the sake of progress in the evolution of humanity.

In the seventh and eighth centuries, for example, there was a very important centre of initiation in the neighbourhood of the Black Sea in which the Buddha taught in his spirit body. In such schools there are those who teach in the physical body; but it is also possible for the more advanced pupils to receive instruction from one who teaches in an etheric body only. And so the Buddha taught pupils there who were capable of receiving higher knowledge. Among the pupils of the Buddha at that time was one who incarnated again a few centuries later. We are speaking, therefore, of a physical personality who centuries later lived again in a physical body, in Italy, and is known to us as St Francis of Assisi. The characteristic quality of Francis of Assisi and of the life of his monks — which has so much similarity with that of the disciples of Buddha — is due to the fact that Francis of Assisi himself was a pupil of Buddha.

It is easy to perceive the contrast between the qualities and characteristics of those who, like Francis of Assisi, were striving fervently for the spirit and those engrossed in the world of industry, technical life and the discoveries of modern civilization. There were many people, including esotericists, who suffered deeply at the thought that in the future two separate classes of human beings would inevitably arise. They foresaw the one class wholly given up to the affairs of practical life, convinced that security depends entirely upon the production of foodstuffs, the construction of machines, and so forth; whereas the other class would be composed of people like Francis of Assisi who withdraw altogether from the practical affairs of the world for the sake of spiritual life.

It was a significant moment, therefore, when Christian Rosenkreutz in the sixteenth century called together a large group of esotericists in preparation for the conference mentioned and described to them the two types of human beings that would inevitably arise in the future. First he gathered a large circle of people, later on a smaller one, to present them with this significant fact. Christian Rosenkreutz held this preparatory meeting a few years beforehand, not because he was in doubt about what would happen, but because he wanted to get people to contemplate future perspectives. In order to stimulate their thinking he spoke roughly as follows: 'Let us look at the future of the world. The world is moving fast in the direction of practical activities, industry, railways, and so on. Human beings will become like beasts of burden. And those who do not want this will be, like Francis of Assisi, impractical in outer life, and will develop an inner life only.' Christian Rosenkreutz made it clear to his listeners that there was no way on earth of preventing these two classes of people from forming. Despite all that might be done for them between birth and death, nothing could prevent humankind being divided into these two classes. As far as earthly conditions are concerned it is impossible to find a remedy for this division into classes. Help could only come if a kind of education arose that did not take place between birth and death but between death and a new birth.

Thus the Rosicrucians faced the task of working from the supersensory world to influence individual human beings. In order to understand what had to take place, we must consider a particular aspect of the life between death and a new birth.

Between birth and death we live on the earth. Between death and a new birth human beings have a certain connection with the other planets. In my *Theosophy* you will find kamaloka described. This stay of the human being in the soul world is a time during which he becomes an inhabitant of the Moon. Then, one after the other, he becomes an inhabitant of Mercury, Venus, the Sun, Mars, Jupiter and Saturn, and then an inhabitant of the further expanses of heaven or the cosmos.[31] It is not incorrect to say that between two incarnations on the earth lie lives on other planets, spiritual incarnations. Man at present is not yet sufficiently developed to remember, whilst in incarnation, his experiences between death and a new birth, but this will become possible in the future. Even though he cannot now remember what he experienced on Mars, for example, he still has Mars forces within him, although he knows nothing about them. We are justified in saying: 'I am an earth inhabitant, but the forces within me include something that I acquired on Mars.'

Let us consider those who lived on earth after the Copernican world outlook had become common knowledge. From where did Copernicus, Galileo, Giordano Bruno and others acquire their abilities? Bear in mind that shortly before that, from 1401 to 1464, the individuality of Copernicus was incarnated as Nicholas of Cusa, a profound mystic. Think of the completely different mood of his *docta ignorantia* or 'learned ignorance'. How did the forces that made Copernicus so very different from Nicholas of Cusa enter this individuality? The forces that made him the astronomer he was came to him from the Mars sphere.[32] Similarly, Galileo also received forces from Mars that invested him with the special configuration of a modern natural scientist. Giordano Bruno, too, brought his powers with him from Mars, and so it was with the whole of mankind. That people think like Copernicus or Giordano Bruno is due to the Mars forces they acquire between death and a new birth.

But the acquisition of the kind of powers which lead from one conquest to another is due to the fact that Mars had a different influence in those times from the one it exercised previously. Mars used to radiate different forces. The Mars culture that human beings experience between death and a new birth went through a great crisis in the earth's fifteenth and sixteenth centuries. It was as decisive and catastrophic a time on Mars in the fifteenth and sixteenth century as it was on the earth at the time of the Mystery of Golgotha. Just as at the time of the Mystery of Golgotha the actual ego of man was born, there was born on Mars that particular tendency which, in man, comes to expression in Copernicanism. When these conditions came into force on Mars, the natural consequence would have been for Mars to continue sending down to earth human beings who only brought Copernican ideas with them, which are really only *maya*. What we are seeing, then, is the decline of Mars culture. Previously Mars had sent forth good forces. But now Mars sent forth more and more forces that would have led us deeper and deeper into *maya*. The achievements inspired by Mars at that time were ingenious and clever, but they were *maya* all the same.

So you see that in the fifteenth century you could have said Mars' salvation, and the earth's too, depended on the declining culture of Mars receiving a fresh impulse to raise it up again. Things were somewhat similar on Mars to how they had been on the earth before the Mystery of Golgotha, when humanity had fallen from spiritual heights into the depths of materialism, and the Christ impulse had signified an ascent. In the fifteenth century it had become necessary for Mars culture to receive an upward impulse. That was the significant question facing Christian Rosenkreutz and his pupils—how this upward impulse could be given to Mars culture, for the salvation of the earth was also at stake. Rosicrucianism was faced with the mighty task of solving the problem of what must happen so that, for the earth's sake, the path of Mars culture should ascend once more. The beings on Mars were not in a position to know what would bring about their salvation, for the earth was the only place where one could know what the situation on Mars was like. On Mars itself they were unaware of the decline.

Therefore it was in order to find a practical solution to this problem that the conference met at the end of the sixteenth century. This conference was well prepared by Christian Rosenkreutz through the fact that his closest friend and pupil was Gautama Buddha, living in a spiritual body. And it was announced at this conference that the being who incarnated as Gautama Buddha, in the spiritual form he now had since becoming Buddha, would transfer the scene of his activities to Mars. The individuality of Gautama Buddha was sent by Christian Rosenkreutz from the earth to Mars. So Gautama Buddha left the scene of his activity and went to Mars, and in the year 1604 the individuality of Gautama Buddha accomplished for Mars a deed similar to what the Mystery of Golgotha signified for the earth. Christian Rosenkreutz had known what the effect of Buddha on Mars would mean for the whole cosmos, what his teachings of *nirvana*, of liberation from the earth, would signify on Mars. The teaching of *nirvana* was unsuited to a form of culture directed primarily to practical life. Buddha's pupil, Francis of Assisi, was an example of the fact that this teaching produces in its adepts profound remoteness from the world and its affairs. But the content of Buddhism, which was not adapted to the practical life of man between birth and death, was of great importance for the soul between death and a new birth. Christian Rosenkreutz realized that for a certain purification needed on Mars the teachings of Buddha were pre-eminently suitable.

As the Christ Being, the essence of divine love, had once come down to the earth to a people in many respects alien to his being, so in the seventeenth century Buddha, the prince of peace, went to Mars — the planet of war and conflict — to execute his mission there. The souls on Mars were warlike, torn with strife. Thus Buddha performed a deed of sacrifice similar to the deed performed in the Mystery of Golgotha by the bearer of the essence of divine love. To dwell on Mars as Buddha was a deed of sacrifice offered to the cosmos. He was what we might describe as the lamb offered up in sacrifice on Mars; to accept this environment of strife was for him a kind of crucifixion. Buddha performed this deed on Mars in the service of Christian Rosenkreutz. Thus do the great beings who guide the world work together not only on the earth but from one planet to another.

Since the Mars Mystery was consummated by Gautama Buddha, human beings have been able during the period between death and a new birth to receive from Mars different forces from those emanating during Mars' cultural decline. Not only does a person bring with him into a new birth quite different forces from Mars, but because of the influence exercised by the spiritual deed of Buddha, forces also stream from Mars into those who practise meditation as a means of reaching the spiritual world. When the modern pupil of spiritual science meditates in the sense proposed by Christian Rosenkreutz, forces sent to the earth by Buddha as the redeemer of Mars stream to him.

Christian Rosenkreutz is thus revealed to us as the great servant of Christ Jesus; but what Buddha, as the emissary of Christian Rosenkreutz, was destined to contribute to the work of Christ Jesus had also to come to the aid of Christian Rosenkreutz's work in the service of Christ Jesus. The soul of Gautama Buddha has not again been in physical incarnation on the earth but is utterly dedicated to the work of the Christ impulse. What was the message of peace sent forth from the Buddha to the Jesus child, described in the Gospel of St Luke? 'Glory in the heights and on the earth — peace!' And this message of peace, issuing mysteriously from Buddha, resounds from the planet of war and conflict to human souls on earth.

Because all these things had transpired, it was possible to avert the division of human beings into the two distinct classes, consisting on the one hand of people such as Francis of Assisi, and on the other of people living wholly materialistic lives. If Buddha had remained in direct and immediate connection with the earth, he would not have been able to concern himself with the 'practical' people, and his influence would have made the others into monks like Francis of Assisi. Through the deed of redemption performed by Gautama Buddha on Mars, it is possible for us, when we are passing through the Mars period of existence between death and a new birth, to become followers of Francis of Assisi without causing subsequent deprivation to the earth. Grotesque as it may seem, it is nevertheless true that since the seventeenth century every human being is a Buddhist, a Franciscan, an immediate follower of Francis of Assisi for a time, whilst he is on Mars. Francis of Assisi has subsequently only had one brief incarnation on earth as a child; and he died in childhood and has not incarnated since. From then onwards he has been connected with the work of Buddha on Mars and is one of his most eminent followers.

We have thus placed before our souls a picture of what came to pass through that great conference at the end of the sixteenth century, which resembles what happened on earth in the thirteenth century when Christian Rosenkreutz gathered his faithful around him. Nothing less was accomplished than averting the danger of humanity separating into two classes; thus human beings could remain inwardly united. And those who want to develop esoterically despite their absorption in practical life can achieve their goal because the Buddha is working from the sphere of Mars and not from the sphere of the earth. Those forces which help to promote a healthy esoteric life can therefore also be attributed to the work and influence of Buddha.

In my book *How To Know Higher Worlds* I have dealt with the methods appropriate for meditation today. The essential point is that in Rosicrucian training the human being is not torn away from the earthly activities which his karma requires of him. Rosicrucian esoteric development can proceed without causing the slightest hindrance in any situation or occupation in life. Because Christian Rosenkreutz was capable of transferring the work of Buddha from the earth to Mars it has become possible for Buddha to exert the right influence on people from beyond the earth.

Again, then, we have heard of one of the spiritual deeds of Christian Rosenkreutz; but to understand these deeds of the thirteenth and sixteenth centuries we must find our way to their esoteric meaning and significance. It would be good if it were generally realized how entirely consistent the progress of theosophy in the West has been since the founding of the Central European section of the Theosophical Society. Here in Switzerland we have had lecture cycles on the four Gospels. The substance of all these Gospel cycles is contained in germinal form in my book *Christianity as Mystical Fact*, written twelve years ago.[33] The book *How To Know Higher Worlds* describes the western path of development that is compatible with practical activities of every kind.

Today I showed that a basic factor in these matters is the mission assigned to Gautama Buddha by Christian Rosenkreutz, by describing the significant influence which the transference of Buddha to Mars made possible in our solar system. And so stone after stone fits into its proper place in our western theosophy, for it has been built up in an inwardly consistent way; and everything that comes later harmonizes with what went before. Inner consistency is essential in any world view if it is to be based on truth. And those who are able to draw near to Christian Rosenkreutz see with reverent wonder the consistent way he has carried out the great mission entrusted to him, which in our time is that of Rosicrucian Christianity. That the great teacher of *nirvana* is now fulfilling a mission outside the earth on Mars — this too is one of the wise and consistent deeds of Christian Rosenkreutz.

A concluding observation

In conclusion, the following brief practical observation will be added for those who aspire to become pupils of Christian Rosenkreutz.

We have already heard how we may gain involuntary knowledge of having a certain relationship to Christian Rosenkreutz. It is also possible, however, to put a kind of question to one's own destiny: 'Can I make myself worthy to become a pupil of Christian Rosenkreutz?' It can come about in the following way. Try to place before your soul a picture of Christian Rosenkreutz, the great teacher of the modern age, in the midst of the twelve, sending forth Gautama Buddha into the cosmos as his emissary at the beginning of the seventeenth century, thus bringing about a consummation of what came to pass in the sixth century BC through the sermon at Benares. If this picture in all its significance stands vividly before the soul, if one feels that something streaming from this great and impressive picture compels the soul to say: 'O human being, you are not merely an earthly being; you are in truth a cosmic being!' — then one may rightly say and believe: 'I can aspire to become a pupil of Christian Rosenkreutz.' This picture of the relationship of Christian Rosenkreutz to Gautama Buddha is a potent and effective meditation. And I wanted to awaken this aspiration in you as a consequence of what has here been described. For our ideal should always be to take an interest in the world, and then to find the way, through such study, to carry out our own development towards higher worlds.

Appendix: The Question of 'Rosicrucian' Literature

An attempt to describe what is expressed in *The Chymical Wedding of Christian Rosenkreutz* entirely through consideration of its content as revealed to the author forms the history of the foregoing pages. It should confirm the judgement that in this text, published by Johann Valentin Andreae, is shown the direction that must be followed when we attempt to understand the true character of higher knowledge. And the present explanations seek to make clear that in *The Chymical Wedding* we have a picture of the special kind of spiritual knowledge required since the fifteenth century. For those who understand Andreae's publication as it is understood by the author of this book, it represents an historical account of a European spiritual stream going back to the fifteenth century, a stream seeking to acquire knowledge about the relationship between all the things which lie behind the phenomena of the external world.

There exists a fairly extensive literature concerning the effect of the work of Johann Valentin Andreae, which discusses whether his published writings can be regarded as actual proof of the existence of a spiritual stream of this nature. In these writings, this stream is indicated to be that of Rosicrucianism. Certain researchers consider the whole affair of Andreae and his Rosicrucian writings simply to be a literary joke intended to ridicule the sentimentality to be found wherever the mysteries of higher knowledge are discussed. From this point of view, Rosicrucianism would be a fantasy created by Andreae for the express purpose of making fun of the wild talk of sentimentalists or of fraudulent mystics.

The author of these pages considers it unnecessary to trouble his readers with a great deal of what is put forward in this way against the seriousness of Andreae's intentions, because he is of the opinion that a correct study of the content of *The Chymical Wedding* provides sufficient basis for understanding what it means to convey. Evidence based on material other than these contents can have no effect upon this opinion. Someone who recognizes the full weight of such internal evidence will evaluate the external documentary evidence on the basis of these internal reasons, and not evaluate the internal on the basis of the external. Therefore if what is said here makes no specific reference to the purely historical literature concerning Rosicrucianism, no adverse criticism of historical research is intended. All that is intended here is that the point of view taken in this exposition makes a full discussion of Rosicrucian literature unnecessary. Let us therefore add only a few remarks.

It is a known fact that the manuscript of *The Chymical Wedding* was completed by 1603. It first made its public appearance in 1616 after Andreae had published his other Rosicrucian document, *Fama Fraternitatis R.C.*, in 1614. It was this publication above all that gave rise to the belief that Andreae's reference to the existence of a Rosicrucian Society was a spoof. This belief was later supported by Andreae's own statement that Rosicrucianism was not a thing he would have cared to defend. There is much in his later writings and in his letters to support the interpretation that his sole purpose was to invent stories concerning this spiritual stream for the mystification of fanatics and the curious. In making use of such evidence, the misunderstandings to which works like those of Andreae are exposed are as a rule ignored. What he himself later said about this can be interpreted correctly only when one realizes that he was obliged to speak in that manner after enemies appeared who severely condemned this spiritual movement as heresy; that adherents had come forward who were fanatical or were alchemical swindlers, distorting everything for which Rosicrucianism stood. But even if all this is taken into consideration, if one is willing to accept the idea that Andreae, who appears later as a Pietistic writer, declined to acknowledge as his what was expressed in the Rosicrucian writings soon after their publication, such considerations still do not provide a sufficiently well-grounded view on the relationship of this personality to Rosicrucianism. Indeed, even if one is willing to go so far as to deny Andreae the authorship of the *Fama*, one cannot on historical grounds do so with regard to *The Chymical Wedding*.

There is also another point of view from which the matter must be considered historically. The *Fama Fraternitatis* appeared in 1614. We can initially leave aside the question whether with this work Andreae wished to approach serious readers to tell them about the spiritual path known as

Rosicrucianism. But *The Chymical Wedding*, which had already been completed 13 years earlier, was published two years after the appearance of the *Fama*. In 1603 Andreae was still a very young man (17 years of age). Are we to suppose that he was sufficiently mature to have let loose a phantom among the sentimentalists of his day by presenting them with Rosicrucianism, a reflection of his power of imagination, as a spoof with which to mock them? Besides, if in the *Fama*, which was being read in manuscript form in the Tyrol as early as 1610, he wished to speak of Rosicrucianism in a serious way, how was it that as a quite young man he composed a document in *The Chymical Wedding* that he published as information concerning true Rosicrucianism two years after the *Fama*? In fact, the questions about Andreae seem to become so entangled that this complicates any purely historical solution. There would be no reason to object if any purely historical researcher tried to argue that Andreae may have found the manuscripts of *The Chymical Wedding* and the *Fama* — perhaps in the possession of his family — and that he published them for some reason in his youth but later repudiated the spiritual views expressed in them. Were this a fact, however, why did not Andreae simply announce that this was the case?

With the help of the science of the spirit one can reach a totally different conclusion. There is no need to connect the content of *The Chymical Wedding* with Andreae's age at the time he wrote it, nor with his powers of judgement. As far as the content is concerned, this document shows itself to be written on the basis of intuition. It is possible for things of this kind to be written down by people with a certain aptitude for them, even if their own powers of judgement and experience in life take no part in what is thus written. And what is written down can nevertheless convey full reality. On the basis of its content one is compelled to accept *The Chymical Wedding* as a communication about an actually existing spiritual current. The assumption that Valentin Andreae wrote it out of intuition sheds a light upon the attitude towards Rosicrucianism he adopted later. As a young man he had the capacity to provide a picture of this spiritual current without using his own source of knowledge. Andreae's own path of knowledge found its development later when he became the Pietistic theologian, whereas the spiritual receptiveness that could reflect intuition receded in his soul.

Later he himself philosophized about what he had written in his youth. He did this as early as 1619 in his *Turris Babel* (Tower of Babel). The connection between the later Andreae and the Andreae who wrote out of intuition in his youth did not become clear to him. If we consider Andreae's attitude towards the content of *The Chymical Wedding* from this perspective, we must treat the content of the document separately without reference to anything expressed by him at any time concerning his connections with Rosicrucianism. What it was possible to reveal about this spiritual stream in Andreae's day was written by a personality able to do so. Whoever believes from the outset that it is impossible for the spiritual life as it takes effect in cosmic phenomena to be revealed in such a way as this will certainly reject what is said here. There may be people, however, who, without superstitious prejudices, will quietly consider the 'case of Andreae', and through it become convinced that this kind of revelation is possible.

Notes

1 The main Rosicrucian texts are available with commentary and extracts from Rudolf Steiner in: Paul M. Allen (ed.), *A Christian Rosenkreutz Anthology* (New York 1968).

2 W.B. Yeats, 'The Mountain Tomb'.

3 Yates, *The Rosicrucian Enlightenment* (London 1993).

4 Steiner, *Mystery Knowledge and Mystery Centres* (London 1997), pp. 102ff (on the mysteries of Ephesus); pp. 211ff (Rosicrucianism).

5 B.J. Teeter Dobbs, *The Hunting of the Green Lion* (Cambridge 1975); M.C. Jacob, *The Radical Enlightenment* (London 2001).

6 See also Suggested Further Reading at the end of this book.

7 Steiner, *Occult Science* (London 1969), pp. 28–30. (New edition: *An Outline of Esoteric Science*, New York 1997.)

8 See W. Pehnt, *Expressionist Architecture* (1998).

9 H. Wiesberger, Introduction to Rudolf Steiner, *Zur Geschichte und aus den Inhalten der erkenntniskultischen Abteilung der esoterischen Schule* (Dornach 1987), pp. 46–64 for a fundamentally balanced survey of Steiner's activities in this sphere. (The attempt to associate Steiner with subsequent developments such as the so-called Ordo Templi Orientis, which is sometimes made on the basis of this connection, suffers at the very least from such acute chronological difficulties—in fact distorts history in so many ways that no serious rebuttal is really necessary.)

10 Steiner, *Autobiography* (New York 1999); Welburn, 'Yeats, the Rosicrucians and Rudolf Steiner', in *Journal for Anthroposophy*, 47 (1988), 28–45; 48 (1988), 51–60.

11   Steiner, *Zur Geschichte und aus den Inhalten der ersten Abteilung der esoterischen Schule* (Dornach 1984), pp. 206ff (and Introduction, pp. 30ff).

12   Steiner, *The Gospel of St Matthew* (London 1986), p. 125. For an approach to esoteric training along these lines, see Rudolf Steiner, *How to Know Higher Worlds: A Modern Path of Initiation* (New York 1994).

13   Steiner, *The True Nature of the Second Coming* (London 1971).

14   'Inspired cognition shows,' says Steiner, 'that as soon after death as someone has watched their life-tableau which ... lasts two or three to four days, their memories dissolve into the cosmos, spreading themselves out there. This experience is often referred to as the freeing of the etheric body.' *Evolution of Consciousness* (London 1966), pp. 122–3. See in general *Occult Science* (London 1969), pp. 69ff.

15   In his incarnation as the Comte de Saint-Germain; cf. the editor's note 27 in Steiner, *Esoteric Christianity and the Mission of Christian Rosenkreutz* (London 2000), pp. 317–8.

16   The original text and an English translation of this work are contained in Paul M. Allen (ed.), *A Christian Rosenkreutz Anthology* (New York 1968), pp. 211–327. The author's extraordinary name is usually taken to be an anagram of Hadrianus a Munsicht, i.e. Mynsicht, a writer of the early seventeenth century.

17   Beginning in AD 1415.

18   No more specific reference to this locality is known.

19   'The power that could go out from these seven great teachers to human beings ... was tremendous. By virtue of their etheric and astral bodies that had been bequeathed to them, with high spiritual forces, the rishis were also able to work magically on their pupils. They did not really teach; they worked as though

by magic from person to person. Thus arose a civilization deeply permeated by supersensory wisdom...': Steiner, *Occult Science*, p. 203.

20 See Rudolf Steiner, *'The Mysteries' (Die Geheimnisse) A Christmas and Easter Poem by Goethe* (London 1946); now reprinted in Steiner, *The Secret Stream* (New York 2000).

21 Cf. Isabel Cooper-Oakley, *The Comte de Saint-Germain* (London 1985).

22 See Rudolf Steiner, *The Reappearance of Christ in the Etheric* (New York 1983).

23 Brother Mark, the character in Goethe's poem whose arrival at a Rosicrucian mystery centre is described. See note 20 above.

24 See Paul M. Allen, *Vladimir Soloviev* (New York 1978); also Eugenia Gourvitch, *Soloviev. The Man and the Prophet* (London 1992).

25 See further Steiner, *Alchemy, The Evolution of the Mysteries* (Sussex 2001).

26 Alchemist, best known for his *Amphitheatre of Eternal Wisdom* (1609).

27 For more on Andreae and the literary problem of *The Chymical Wedding*, see also the Appendix at the end of this book.

28 For this passage in *The Chymical Wedding* see Paul M. Allen (ed.), *A Christian Rosenkreutz Anthology*, p. 159.

29 'Luciferic' influence is to be understood in Rudolf Steiner's work as one form of unbalanced spirituality, the polar opposite to that of Ahriman, or unbalanced tendency to materialism.

    Luciferic abstract ideas such as often find a place in science actually tend to make us lose contact with the full experience of nature. Spiritual science wishes to find higher truth, but also to retain the richness of experience.

30   Luke 2:14. See further Steiner, *The Gospel of Luke* (London 1964), pp. 39ff.

31   See Rudolf Steiner, *Theosophy*, chapter III. Also his lectures *Between Death and Rebirth* (London 1975).

32   The terms moon, Mars, etc. are used in an occult sense to denote spiritual domains. By Mars Steiner does not mean the physical planet, but a vast sphere corresponding physically to the globe defined by the physical planet's orbit. This region is among those traversed by the soul after death. Only when the spiritual meaning was lost did the names Mars etc. come to be used in a material sense. Cf. Steiner, *The Spiritual Hierarchies* (New York 1970), lecture 1.

33   See especially *The Gospel of John* (New York 1962); also Steiner's *Christianity as Mystical Fact* (New York 1997).

Sources

This book comprises thematic extracts from the lectures and writings of Rudolf Steiner.

'The mystery of Christian Rosenkreutz' reproduces pp. 45–56 of the lectures *Esoteric Christianity and the Mission of Christian Rosenkreutz* (London 2000), translated from GA 130 in the edition of Rudolf Steiner's original works.

'The working of Christian Rosenkreutz — then and today' reproduces pp. 254–60 and pp. 59–61 in the same volume.

'Christian Rosenkreutz as the guardian of modern knowledge' reproduces pp. 61–7 from the same volume, followed by pp. 49–56 from Rudolf Steiner's essay 'The Chymical Wedding of Christian Rosenkreutz' in Paul M. Allen (ed.), *A Christian Rosenkreutz Anthology* (New York 1968).

'The cosmic mission of Christian Rosenkreutz' reproduces pp. 283–94 from *Esoteric Christianity and the Mission of Christian Rosenkreutz*.

The Appendix reproduces pp. 56–9 from Rudolf Steiner's essay 'The Chymical Wedding of Christian Rosenkreutz' in Paul M. Allen (ed.), *A Christian Rosenkreutz Anthology*.

Translations by Carlo Pietzner and Pauline Wehrle.

Suggested Further Reading

Allen, P.M., *A Christian Rosenkreutz Anthology* (New York 1968)

Bennell, M. and Wyatt, I., *An Introductory Commentary on the Chymical Wedding* (Stroud n.d.)

By Rudolf Steiner:

Christianity as Mystical Fact (New York 1997)

Esoteric Christianity and the Mission of Christian Rosenkreutz (London 2000)

From Jesus to Christ (London 1973)

The Gospel of Luke (London 1964)

Guidance in Esoteric Training (London 1998)

How to Know Higher Worlds (New York 1984)

Occult Science (London 1969). Also available as *An Outline of Esoteric Science* (New York 1997)

Occult Signs and Symbols (New York 1972)

Rosicrucian Esotericism (New York 1972)

Rosicrucianism and Modern Initiation (London 1982)

The Secret Stream (New York 2000)

The Spiritual Foundation of Morality (Vancouver n.d.)

The Temple Legend (London 1985)

Theosophy of the Rosicrucian (London 1981)

A Vision for the Millennium (London 1999)

Note Regarding Rudolf Steiner's Lectures

The lectures and addresses contained in this volume have been translated from the German, which is based on stenographic and other recorded texts that were in most cases never seen or revised by the lecturer. Hence, due to human errors in hearing and transcription, they may contain mistakes and faulty passages. Every effort has been made to ensure that this is not the case. Some of the lectures were given to audiences more familiar with anthroposophy; these are the so-called 'private' or 'members' lectures. Other lectures, like the written works, were intended for the general public. The difference between these, as Rudolf Steiner indicates in his *Autobiography*, is twofold. On the one hand, the members' lectures take for granted a background in and commitment to anthroposophy; in the public lectures this was not the case. At the same time, the members' lectures address the concerns and dilemmas of the members, while the public work speaks directly out of Steiner's own understanding of universal needs. Nevertheless, as Rudolf Steiner stresses: 'Nothing was ever said that was not solely the result of my direct experience of the growing content of anthroposophy. There was never any question of concessions to the prejudices and preferences of the members. Whoever reads these privately printed lectures can take them to represent anthroposophy in the fullest sense. Thus it was possible without hesitation — when the complaints in this direction became too persistent — to depart from the custom of circulating this material "For members only". But it must be borne in mind that faulty passages do occur in these reports not revised by myself.' Earlier in the same chapter, he states: 'Had I been able to correct them [the private lectures], the restriction *for members only* would have been unnecessary from the beginning.'

The original German editions on which this text is based were published by Rudolf Steiner Verlag, Dornach, Switzerland in the collected edition (*Gesamtausgabe*, 'GA') of Rudolf Steiner's work. All publications are edited by the Rudolf Steiner Nachlassverwaltung (estate), which wholly owns both Rudolf Steiner Verlag and the Rudolf Steiner Archive. The organization relies solely on donations to continue its activity.

For further information please contact:

Rudolf Steiner Archiv
Postfach 135
CH-4143 Dornach

or:

www.rudolf-steiner.com

ALSO AVAILABLE IN THE 'POCKET LIBRARY OF SPIRITUAL WISDOM' SERIES

Rudolf Steiner
Alchemy
The Evolution of the Mysteries

Alchemy and the Rise of the Modern Mysteries; The Loss of the Divine and the Alchemical Quest; Mysteries of the Metals; The Standpoint of Human Wisdom Today; Alchemy and Consciousness—the Transformation; Alchemy and Archangels; The Alchemy of Nature—Mercury, Sulphur, Salt; Beyond Nature Consciousness—the Spiritual Goal.

RSP; 112pp; 17 × 12 cm; 1 85584 089 8; pb; £7.95

Rudolf Steiner
Atlantis
The Fate of a Lost Land and its Secret Knowledge

The Continent of Atlantis; The Moving Continents; The
History of Atlantis; The Earliest Civilizations; The
Beginnings of Thought; Etheric Technology – Atlantean
'Magic' Powers; Twilight of the Magicians; The Divine
Messengers; Atlantean Secret Knowledge – it's Betrayal and
Subsequent Fate; The Origins of the Mysteries; Atlantis and
Spiritual Evolution.

RSP; 112pp; 17 × 12 cm; 1 85584 079 0; pb; £7.95

Rudolf Steiner
The Druids
Esoteric Wisdom of the Ancient Celtic Priests

The Sun Initiation of the Druid Priests and their Moon
Science; The Mysteries of Ancient Ireland; Celtic
Christianity — the Heritage of the Druids; Teachings of the
Mysteries — the Spirit in Nature; The Great Mysteries — the
Mystery of Christ; The Function of the Standing Stones;
Spiritual Imaginations.

RSP; 96pp; 17 × 12 cm; 1 85584 099 5; pb; £7.95

Rudolf Steiner
The Goddess
From Natura to the Divine Sophia

Rediscovering the Goddess Natura; Retracing our Steps —
Mediaeval Thought and the School of Chartres; The Goddess
Natura in the Ancient Mysteries; The Goddess in the
Beginning — the Birth of the Word; Esoteric Christianity — the
Virgin Sophia; the Search for the New Isis; The Renewal of
the Mysteries; The Modern Isis, the Divine Sophia.

RSP; 112pp; 17 × 12 cm; 1 85584 094 4; pb; £7.95

Rudolf Steiner
The Holy Grail
The Quest for the Renewal of the Mysteries

From the Mysteries to Christianity; Death and Resurrection
in Ancient Egypt—the Miracle of Initiation; The Mystery of
Golgotha; The Mystery of the Higher Ego—the Holy Grail;
The Grail and the Spiritual Evolution of Humanity; The
Gnostic Crisis and the Loss of the Mysteries; Stages of
Evolution—Archaic Clairvoyance; The Role of the Mysteries;
The Secret of Evolution—the Holy Grail.

RSP; 96pp; 17 × 12 cm; 1 85584 074 X; pb; £7.95